A Note to Parents

DK READERS is a compelling program for beginning readers, designed in conjunction with leading literacy experts, including Dr. Linda Gambrell, Distinguished Professor of Education at Clemson University. Dr. Gambrell has served as President of the National Reading Conference, the College Reading Association, and the International Reading Association.

Beautiful illustrations and superb full-color photographs combine with engaging, easy-to-read stories to offer a fresh approach to each subject in the series. Each DK READER is guaranteed to capture a child's interest while developing his or her reading skills, general knowledge, and love of reading.

The five levels of DK READERS are aimed at different reading abilities, enabling you to choose the books that are exactly right for your child:

Pre-level 1: Learning to read
Level 1: Beginning to read
Level 2: Beginning to read alone
Level 3: Reading alone
Level 4: Proficient readers

The "normal" age at which a child begins to read can be anywhere from three to eight years old. Adult participation through the lower levels is very helpful for providing encouragement, discussing storylines, and sounding out unfamiliar words.

No matter which level you select, you can be sure that you are helping your child learn to read, then read to learn!

LONDON, NEW YORK, MUNICH,
MELBOURNE, and DELHI

Series Editor Deborah Lock
US Senior Editor Shannon Beatty
Project Art Editor Hoa Luc
Producer, Pre-production Francesca Wardell

Reading Consultant
Linda Gambrell, Ph.D.

DK DELHI
Editor Pomona Zaheer
Assistant Art Editor Yamini Panwar
DTP Designer Anita Yadav
Picture Researcher Surya Sarangi
Deputy Managing Editor Soma B. Chowdhury

First American Edition, 2014
Published in the United States by DK Publishing
345 Hudson Street, New York, New York 10014

14 15 16 17 10 9 8 7 6 5 4 3 2 1
001–253406–August/2014

A catalog record for this book is available
from the Library of Congress.

ISBN: 978-1-4654-2009-1 (Paperback)
ISBN: 978-1-4654-2008-4 (Hardcover)

DK books are available at special discounts when purchased in bulk
for sales promotions, premiums, fund-raising, or educational use.
For details, contact:
DK Publishing Special Markets
345 Hudson Street, New York, New York 10014
SpecialSales@dk.com

Printed and bound in China by
South China Printing Company

The publisher would like to thank the following
for their kind permission to reproduce their photographs:
(Key: a=above, b=below/bottom, c=center, l=left, r=right, t=top)
10 Alamy Images: GM Photo Images (c). 11 Alamy Images: Sue Cunningham/
Worldwide Picture Library (t). 13 Alamy Images: Andrew Paterson (ftr); ImageDB/
PhotosIndia.com LLC (tr); Corbis: Susanne Borges/A.B. (c); Dreamstime.com: Jo
Ann Snover (fcra). 14 Alamy Images: Andrew Twort (cr); Corbis: Konrad Wothe/
Minden Pictures (c). 15 Alamy Images: Morley Read (t). 17 Corbis: Jeffrey Bosdet/
All Canada Photos (b). 18 Corbis: Top Photo Group (t). 19 Corbis: Gordon
Wiltsie/National Geographic Society (b). 21 Alamy Images: Realimage (crb);
Nigel Hicks (b). 22 Corbis: Sung-IL Kim/Sung-Il Kim (t). 23 Dorling Kindersley:
Rough Guides (ca). 25 Dorling Kindersley: Laszlo Veres. 27 Corbis: Kevin
Schafer (b). 28 Dorling Kindersley: Thomas Marent (tl, tr). 31 Alamy Images:
Bruce Farnsworth (b). 32 Alamy Images: Graphic Science (t). 33 Alamy Images:
Interfoto/Botany (c). 34 Alamy Images: Krys Bailey (c). 35 Alamy Images: Ton
Koene/Horizons WWP (b). 36 Alamy Images: Bob Masters (t). 37 Alamy Images:
Frans Lemmens (t). 39 Corbis: Kevin Schafer (ca). 40 Alamy Images: Ammit (t).
42 Alamy Images: David Wall (c). 43 Alamy Images: ZUMA Press, Inc. (t).
44 Alamy Images: Maxime Dube (b). 45 Alamy Images: Maxime Dube (t).
Jacket images: Front: Corbis: Gyro Photography/Amanaimages (t); Dreamstime.
com: Janpietruszka; Back: Dorling Kindersley: Rough Guides

All other images © Dorling Kindersley
For further information see: www.dkimages.com

Discover more at
www.dk.com

Contents

Rain Forest Explorer

Written by Rupert Matthews

Amazonian Blog
Day 1 My arrival
Posted by Zoe Dorado

I am exhausted! But I am also very excited. I have arrived in Boa Vista in Brazil and have met my Uncle Renaldo. We are getting ready to go to Uncle Renaldo's Rain Forest Research Station. Uncle Renaldo is studying the animals in northern Brazil. He wants to find out if the number of animals is decreasing because of the loss of rain forest.

4

I am looking forward to helping
him with the research.

Map to the Research Station

Key

 By airplane

 By boat

 On foot

- - - - - - - Route

● Belém City

● Boa Vista village

● Research Station

Here is how to pronounce some of the place names:

Caracaí [KARA-kie]

Kuhikugu [KOO-ee-koo-goo]

Tulu Tuloi [TOO-loo TOO-loy]

Xeriuini [SHE-ree-oo-eenee]

South America

Brazil

Rio Branco

Rio Negro

Amazon River

Brasilia
(capital of Brazil)

Amazon rain forest

I landed in Brazil at the Val de Cans Airport. Then I continued my journey on a small propeller aircraft, flying to the Boa Vista Airport. On the flight, I read a magazine. One article was about people cutting down the rain forest. The rain forest around the Amazon River is vast, covering 3,500,000 square miles.

However, around 370,000 square miles has already been cut down. That is terrible! The animals' homes are being destroyed and their habitats are getting smaller. The land is being used for farming. I guess the farmers need to live somewhere, too.

Another article was about the strange finds at Kuhikugu. This is a village in the rain forest far to the south of Boa Vista. People there have found the ruins of towns, roads, and ditches that are hundreds of years old. Thousands of people must have lived there once. Today the ruins are covered by rain forest. How mysterious!

Uncle Renaldo met me at the Boa
Vista Airport, which is very small.
He took me to a hotel through
the bustling town of Boa Vista.

We ate a dinner of pato no tucupi.
This is pieces of duck cooked with
grated manioc root.

Manioc, pronounced man-ee-ok, is a bit like a soft potato, and it's a very popular food here. Uncle says that we'll eat it nearly every day.

I have to finish this entry now and upload it to the blog. Then I can go to sleep. I wonder what will happen tomorrow.

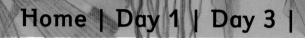

Amazonian Blog
Day 3 Boa Vista
Posted by Zoe Dorado

I have had a busy few days in Boa Vista.
I have packed what I will need for the trip
in a special backpack Uncle Renaldo gave
me. I am ready to go and I can't wait.

Yesterday Uncle introduced me to
his friend Pedro, who is a member
of the Yanomani Amazon tribe.
Uncle Renaldo says we will all leave
very early tomorrow morning.

It will be cool then, but it is hot now.
The thermometer says the temperature
is 100°F (38°C), and it's raining very hard.

12

Sam Browne belt

This is a wide leather belt with several metal rings stitched to it. Things such as a water bottle, knife, notebook, and binoculars can be clipped to the rings.

Head cover

Wearing a canvas hat with a wide brim in the rain forest helps to keep the sun out of the eyes and the rain off.

It rains for about five hours each day. No wonder they call this the "rain forest"!

We plan to travel down the Rio Branco —that means "White River"—toward the town of Caracaí. This river is a tributary of the great Amazon River.

This Rio Branco is actually a mud brown color. It is called the "White River" because there is a Rio Negro—"Black River"—that flows to the south and really is black in color. The Rio Negro looks like strong black tea. Weird!

Amazonian Blog
Day 4 The Rio Branco
Posted by Zoe Dorado

Zoe here—but only just. What an adventure and a narrow escape! Pedro and I went fishing just now to catch something for lunch.
I was sitting on the edge of the canoe with a couple of fish he had caught, when a barge went past. The wave from the barge made the canoe rock and I fell into the water. Uncle Renaldo started shouting. Pedro threw a rope

to me and pulled me out
of the river. Pedro looked
frightened. Uncle Renaldo
kept asking if I was safe.
They both looked very worried.

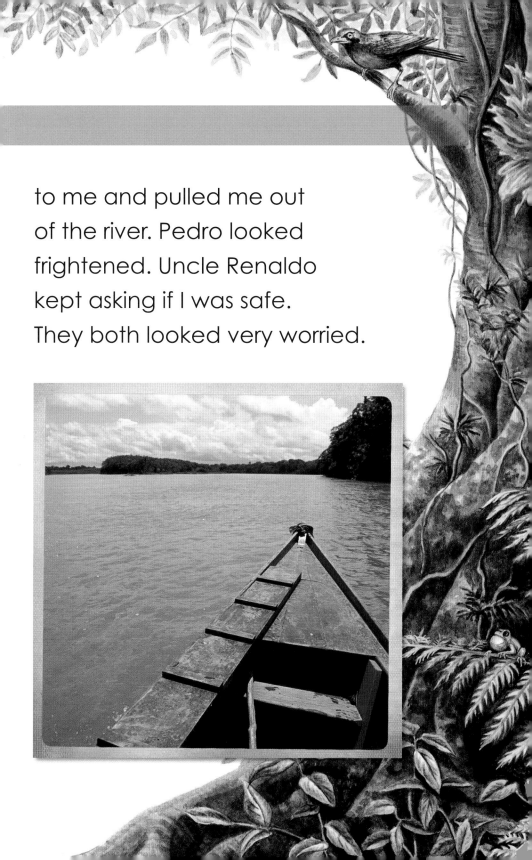

They told me that dangerous
piranha live in the Rio Branco.
Piranha are fish that live in groups
of up to several hundred fish.
If they smell blood in the water,
they will attack and can kill
a person in just a few seconds.
How frightening is that? Uncle
Renaldo is now frying fish and
peas in peanut oil. We will eat this
with boiled manioc.

As we traveled along the river,
we passed several villages.
At one village, a crane was lifting
huge blocks of white stone on to
a barge tied to the river bank.
I recognized this as marble, which
is used to make sculptures or for
building. We also saw barges
carrying copper ore. I was
surprised to see cranes and
mines in the rain forest.

Amazonian Blog
Day 5 In the rain forest
Posted by Zoe Dorado

We are camping beside a small stream in the rain forest. It is raining—again! Uncle Renaldo set up a canvas canopy and lit a fire. We had manioc (of course) with dried peas. I am getting bored with eating manioc—I'd love a burger. We left the canoe in the town of Caracaí, which is much smaller than Boa Vista.

We rode on a truck to the village of Igarape. The farmers in the village grow manioc to eat, as well as soybeans and pineapples that they sell in Caracaí.

20

Walking boots

Leather boots that are tough but comfortable are needed for walking in the rain forest. They lace up above the ankle to give support.

The road is just dirt and gravel.
In places, there were deep
holes filled with water and mud.
All the trees had been cut down
along the sides of the road. Other
roads led off into the forest, and
I noticed that the trees were
being cut down there as well.
There's no road after Igarape—
only paths through the forest.
We began walking after lunch
and walked until almost night.

I was looking for animals, but
I didn't see a single one.

It is very dark here. Even in the middle
of the day, it's gloomy since the huge
leaves and branches overhead block
out nearly all the sunlight. I could
hear animals calling above me, but
I couldn't see any since they were
hidden by the leaves. Perhaps I will
see something tomorrow. Good night.

Amazon Animals

Thousands of different types of animal live in the Amazon rain forest. The rain forest is full of color, sounds, and danger.

1. Amazon ants
There are more than 1,000 different types.

2. Scarlet macaw
This is one of the most colorful parrots.

3. Toucan
Its impressive beak is a third of its length.

4. Jaguar
This powerful hunter can climb and swim.

5. Anaconda
This giant snake can grow to 30 ft (9 m).

6. Capybara
This is the world's largest rodent.

7. Blue morpho butterfly
This insect dazzles with an 8 in. (20 cm) wingspan.

8. Peccary
Its tusks rub together to make a chattering noise.

9. Tapir [TAY-peer]
Its snout is like a short elephant's trunk.

10. Hummingbird
Its rapid wingbeat helps it to hover over flowers.

Amazonian Blog
Day 6 In the rain forest
Posted by Zoe Dorado

Wow! Pedro has just shown me some round marks in the dirt near our tent. They are the footprints of a jaguar, which came to our camp in the night. This big cat can grow to be 6.5 feet (2 meters) long and weigh 330 pounds (150 kilograms). I didn't hear anything, but Pedro says you never hear the jaguar. It moves like a shadow and kills silently, biting into a skull with its long teeth. You are dead before you hear it.

26

Pedro laughed when he told me this and saw the fear on my face. Thankfully, jaguars don't attack humans unless threatened, since we are too dangerous.

Pedro has pointed to other footprints and told me which animals had made them. Now that I know what to look for, I can see signs of animals everywhere.

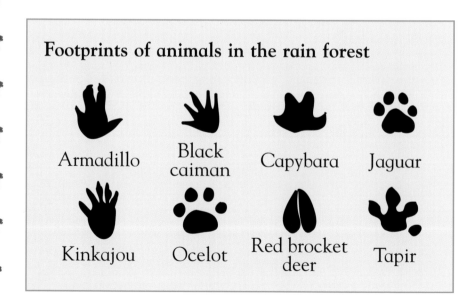

Footprints of animals in the rain forest

Armadillo

Black caiman

Capybara

Jaguar

Kinkajou

Ocelot

Red brocket deer

Tapir

I have found lots of footprints and even seen some birds, frogs, and insects. Today we will climb up into the hills where the forest becomes less dense. Pedro says that there will be bushes and short trees, as well as the giant rain forest trees. We are near Rio Xeriuini and getting close to Pedro's home, Shadea.

Amazonian Blog
Day 9 Tulu Tuloi Hills
Posted by Zoe Dorado

For the last three days, I have been living with the Yanomani tribe. It is great. They are very friendly and have wonderful ways of doing things. We even had a feast!
We are in the village where Pedro comes from. The village centers around a huge wooden house called a shabono. It is shaped like a huge donut, and its roof is made of dried leaves.

About 80 people live inside this shabono. I am staying in a room with two girls my own age—Kara and Haxi.

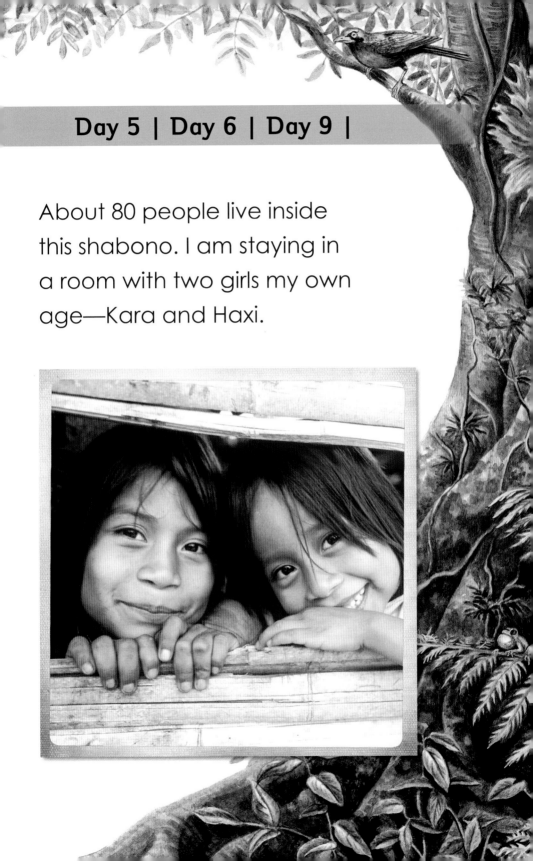

On the first morning, I went out working with Kara and Haxi. We walked to a large mound of hard earth, which was a termite nest. I helped Kara and Haxi to dig out the young termites. They look like fat caterpillars. We ate them fried for lunch, and they tasted a bit like hazelnuts.

In the afternoon, we went to the village garden. This is a clearing in the forest surrounded by a wooden fence to keep out deer and other animals. Women grow different types of plants for food. Kara dug up some manioc roots, while Haxi and I picked bananas.

When we finished, we played a game called olliztli.

Olliztli

This is a board game for two players played with six red counters and six blue counters and a die. Using dice throws, the first player to move his or her counters all the way around the board is the winner.

The men returned from hunting with a capybara and a tapir. There was far too much meat for us to eat, so people from another village were invited to a big feast the next day.

I helped to wash and peel the manioc roots, which I then grated and mixed with some water to form a paste.

A woman then formed the paste into a flat disk about 12 inches (30 centimeters) across. She dropped it on to a hot stone next to a fire. Within a few minutes, the disk puffed up, looking like a bubbly pancake. I took it off the stone and put it in a basket. We cooked dozens of these pancake things.

The feast was a great success.
A group of men played music
on drums and flutes. Everyone
danced and then ate together.
An old tribesman told us stories
about the past. Then there was
more dancing and more eating,
and we went to bed very late.

Tomorrow we must leave the village of Shadea because some people from a nearby tribe are coming to visit. This tribe has never made contact with people from outside the rain forest. They might catch our germs and get sick, or they might think we are invading their land.

Amazonian Blog
Day 22 Research Station
Posted by Zoe Dorado

We reached Uncle Renaldo's Station ten days ago. It is really interesting. Uncle Renaldo has been showing me the work he and Pedro are doing. They have been counting how many of each animal there are. They catch some animals and weigh, measure, and photograph them before letting them go.

This is an armadillo.

But my big news is not about animals. It is about what I found in the rain forest soon after we arrived here. I am thrilled! You will soon see me on television!

Do you remember I told you
about the magazine article
about Kuhikugu? I found
a ditch exactly like the ones
in the magazine. I followed
the ditch through the rain forest,
and it formed a square about
656 feet (200 meters) across.

Near the river were the ruins of a strange structure of stone. It looked a bit like a dam. I took pictures of the ditches and drew a sketch map. I also found large areas of strange black dirt.

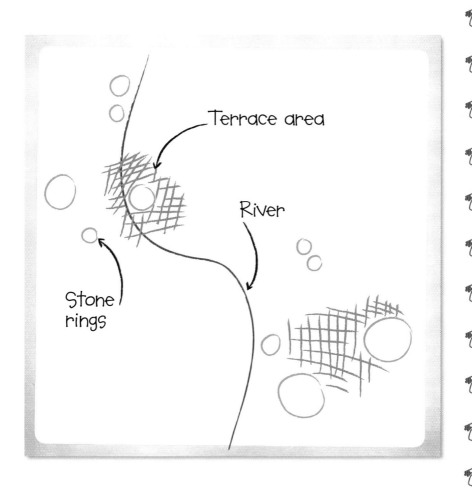

Terrace area

River

Stone rings

Uncle Renaldo sent my findings
over his satellite upload direct
to the National Museum of Brazil.
Two days later, a helicopter arrived.

Professor Gonzales from the
National Museum and a team
of researchers were on board.
They stayed here for several days,
digging holes at the ruins, collecting
things, and taking pictures. Gonzales
and his assistants found several
other ditches and ruins.

Professor Gonzales says he thinks there was a mighty civilization in the Amazon rain forest in the past. Great cities and towns once stood on this site and in other places. He thinks more than 5,000 people lived here then, but new diseases brought by settlers from Europe wiped out the civilization.

Professor Gonzales says my finds are very important. He wants me to go to the National Museum in Brasilia to give a talk about how I found the ruins. Television cameras will be there, so I will be famous around the world. I can hardly wait. How exciting! What a wonderful visit I have had to the rain forest.

Rain Forest Layers

The rain forest is made up of a number of layers of plant life. Different kinds of animals live in different layers of the rain forest.

Emergent

This is made up of a few very tall trees that reach up to 130 ft (40 m) tall. These tall trees emerge from the canopy.

Canopy

This is about 100 ft (30 m) above the ground. The branches of the trees form a solid layer of leaves, branches, and twigs.

Understorey

This is made up of tree trunks and climbing plants. Some birds, lizards, and insects live here.

Forest floor

A few plants, such as ferns or bushes, grow here. There is not enough light for much to grow.

Glossary

Assistant
Person who helps
with some work.

Barge
Long, flat-bottomed
boat that carries
loads along a canal.

Blog
Website where
someone often
writes his or
her thoughts.

Civilization
Developed
community
of people.

Habitat
Home and
surroundings of
a plant or animal.

Professor
Teacher at
a university
or college.

Rodent
A mammal with
incisor teeth that
keep growing, so
it needs to gnaw
constantly.

Satellite
Piece of equipment
that orbits the Earth.

Tributary
River that flows
into a main river.

Index

DK READERS help children learn to read, then read to learn. If you enjoyed this DK READER, then look out for these other titles for your child.

Level 3 African Adventure
Experience the trip of a lifetime on an African safari as recorded in Katie's diary. Share her excitement at seeing wild animals up close.

Level 3 Shark Reef
Blanche, Harry, Ash, and Moby are the sharks who live on the reef. Be entertained by their encounters with the shark visitors that come passing through.

Level 3 LEGO® Friends: Summer Adventures
Enjoy a summer of fun in Heartlake City with Emma, Mia, Andrea, Stephanie, Olivia, and friends.